D1598149

KEYS TO
PERFORMANCE

ACHIEVING EXCELLENCE IN YOUR CAREER AND PERSONAL LIFE.

KEYS TO PERFORMANCE BY JULIO MELARA

ISBN 09642430-3-2
Copyright ©2001 by Julio Melara
Design by James Ware.
Published by Time For Action.

To order more copies of the book or for further information on Julio Melara call toll-free 1.800.355.8463 or log on to juliomelara.com

A WORD TO THE READER

Inside this booklet are 100 keys and insights on topics that affect your performance, productivity, prosperity, potential, protection and possibilities in your life. They have inspired and helped me, and I hope they do the same for you.

I chose to produce a little book that could be easily carried and read at the office or in bed. May you find the keys and insights a rewarding and pleasant companion for a lifetime!

Julio Melara

KEYS TO PERFORMANCE

Index

KEYS TO PERFORMANCE

KEYS TO PERFORMANCE

BELIEF

Doubt is deadly! No person can consistently perform in a manner that is inconsistent with the way they see themselves. All the potential you will ever need is inside you. The wealthiest spot on the planet is not in the oil fields of Kuwait or Saudi Arabia, in the gold or diamond mines of South Africa, the uranium mines of the Soviet Union, or the silver mines of Africa. The richest deposits on earth lie a few blocks and miles away from your house in your local cemetery. Buried beneath the soil are dreams that never came to pass, songs that were never sung, inventions that were never designed, books that were never written, paintings that were never painted, visions that never became a reality and purposes that were never fulfilled. Our cemeteries are filled with potential that merely remained potential. Don't let it happen to you!

TIME

TIME is the currency of life. The franc is the currency of France. The peso is the currency of Mexico. The yen is the currency of Japan. The dollar is the currency of the United States. The currency of life is time. You can be happy and not pay attention to time, but you will not be an achiever. If you are going to succeed in your relationships and career, you have to account for your time. Everyone is given 365 days a year and 24 hours a day. Successful people are different because they accomplish more by managing their priorities, events and opportunities in their time schedule, rather than wasting any of their time. Know the true value of your time—invest, seize and enjoy every moment. Never put off until tomorrow what you can accomplish today!

POSITIVE ATTITUDE

Your mind is the drawing board for tomorrow's circumstances. What happens in your mind can happen in reality. The edge you are looking for today is in your mind. Your attitude can be your greatest asset or liability. Your attitude more than anything else will determine how far you go in life and how much you accomplish. What are you doing on a daily basis to keep your attitude positive? Are you reading something daily that is inspirational, spiritual, positive or motivational? What about the people you associate with? Are they positive or negative influences in your life? Researchers say that the average person has 40,000 thoughts a day and 80 percent are negative. Maintain a positive attitude in a negative world by renewing your mind daily!

SUCCESS

Do you link success to money, power or fame? In 1828, Noah Webster wrote the first dictionary, and he used these four words to define success: Fortunate, prosperous, happy and content. Three of the four adjectives he used to define success had nothing to do with money. And there lies the great dilemma in America today. You like the things money can buy—it can buy you a nice car, suit, house or boat. But you love the things it can't buy. It can't buy you peace, health, love, character, reputation, passion, integrity, tenacity, perseverance or enthusiasm. Success is reaching your maximum potential by being committed to excellence in everything you do and fulfilling God's plan for your life. Remember, success should always be linked to excellence and fulfillment!

<u>RELATIONSHIPS</u>

Every relationship in your life is a current moving you toward your dreams or away from them. Not all friendships should be given the same value. You must recognize which ones are making deposits into your life and which ones are making withdrawals. Which ones increase you and which ones decrease you. Which ones feed you and which ones feed off of you. There are four types of people in your life: those who add, subtract, multiply and divide. Your responsibility is to get away from those who subtract and divide from your life, those who are constantly criticizing, whining and complaining. Get close to those who add and multiply to your life, those who support you, encourage you, pray for you, coach you and even correct you. Avoid relationships with those who do not discern your worth.

SACRIFICE

No matter what you want in life, you are going to have to give up something to get it. Most people are willing to pay $150,000 for a new house, $35,000 for a new car, and $20,000 for a new boat, but very few people are willing to pay the price for success, no matter how much they want it. There is no success without sacrifice. To have a good marriage, to stay in shape or to succeed in business, you will have to sacrifice. You pay a price for everything in life. You pay a price to lose weight. You pay a price to win. You pay a price to get stronger, faster, better. You pay a price for changing, and you even pay a price for staying the same. Can you think of one person in history whose name is worthy of memory who led a life of ease and didn't have to sacrifice anything? What price are you currently paying to attain your goals or dreams? If you are not willing to pay the price for success, you will pay with failure.

ATTITUDE

A few years ago a Fortune 500 study found that 94 percent of all executives surveyed attributed their success more to attitude than any other factor. If you want to go far in your career you must have a good attitude. Your attitude affects more than just your ability to succeed in business. It affects every aspect of your life—even your health. A study was conducted of 57 cancer patients who had undergone mastectomies at King's College Hospital in London, England. Research showed that, of the patients with a positive attitude when they were diagnosed with cancer, 7 out of 10 were still alive 10 years later. But of the patients who felt a sense of hopelessness during diagnosis, 8 out of 10 had died. A good attitude is the fuel that will make your journey down the road of life a long and successful one.

<u>PERSONAL RESPONSIBILITY</u>

I once read a sign that said, "If you could kick the person responsible for most of your troubles, you wouldn't be able to sit down for weeks." Successful people always take responsibility for their own lives, while unsuccessful people duck responsibility. Many people want to blame their problems on their past, their spouse, the government, their customers, their employer, their employees and anyone else they can find. However, the person most responsible for your success can be seen every morning at around 7 a.m. gazing lovingly into the bathroom mirror. Only when you take total responsibility for your life can you look at yourself with honesty, assess your strengths and weaknesses, and begin to change. Remember, when you carry responsibility on your shoulders, there's no room for chips!

GROWTH

Change is inevitable, but growth is optional. There are only three things you can do with change: You can fight it, ignore it or embrace it. If you fight change in your organization or life, you'll become discouraged or discontented and you'll never reach your full potential. If you ignore change, you'll be swept away by your colleagues or competition. However, if you learn to embrace change, mold it and understand that it is part of life, you'll be on your way to enjoying the journey of life. If you can't change, you won't grow, and if you're not growing, you're not really living. How many books have you read this past year? Most people are willing to pay $25 for a good meal, but they won't spend a dime for a good book or a set of tapes that can help them change, improve and learn. When you are through changing, you're through. Growth must be a priority or it will never happen.

INFLUENCE

Influence cannot be asserted; it can only be earned. If you think you've got the same influence with everybody, try telling your best friend's dog what to do. Influence comes from the time you invest, the interest you show, the consistency you demonstrate, and above all, the trustworthiness you exemplify. In other words, influence comes from having integrity; and nothing is more important to your future than personal integrity. Integrity always puts character over personal gain, people over things, service over power, principle over convenience and the long view over the immediate. This means that if your level of influence has been negative or low, you can change. You can become a person of influence who helps others.

LOYALTY

Once, two men were traveling together when suddenly they spied a bear. Before the bear saw them, one of the men ran to a tree, climbed up and hid. The other man was not nearly as nimble as his companion, so he threw himself to the ground and pretended to be dead. The bear sniffed all around the fellow, as he lay there motionless, holding his breath. Finally, after what seemed like an eternity, the bear went away. The traveler in the tree came down and asked his friend what the bear had whispered to him when he put his mouth in his ear. The second man replied, "He told me to never travel with a friend who will leave at the first sign of danger." The parable of the bear is a lesson for the ages. In business, or with family or friends, success cannot be found unless everyone on the team holds to the principle of loyalty.

<u>CHANGE</u>

In 1100 A.D., the following words were inscribed on the tomb of an English bishop in Westminster: "In my youth, my imagination had no limits. I dreamed of changing the world. But as I grew older and wiser, I found that the world would not change, so I decided to change my country. But it, too, seemed immovable. So as I grew into my twilight years, in one last attempt, I settled for changing my family, but they would have none of it. Now on my death bed, I realize that if only I had first changed myself, then by example, I might have changed my family, and through my family changed my country, and through my country changed the world." Novelist Leo Tolstoy once said, "Everyone thinks of changing the world, but no one thinks of changing themselves." Any change you desire should begin with you! In order to change your world, you must change yourself!

FAILING

Most people who are considered highly successful today have failed far more times than they have "won." The game of baseball is a perfect example: Hank Aaron and Babe Ruth both struck out far more times than they got hits or home runs. Thomas Edison failed at his inventions far more times than he succeeded. It's a well-known fact that Walt Disney, Ray Kroc, Bill Gates and many other successful people struggled. Michael Jordan and Larry Bird both missed more shots than they made. Whether in sports, business or parenting, the fact is, you will fall down many times in life. Successful people fail and make mistakes. However, they never give up. They take responsibility for their actions. They don't blame the past, their family or anyone else. When they fall down, they dust themselves off, get back up and continue to pursue their goals. Do you? Remember, only those who are willing to endure the pain of the struggle will ultimately enjoy the rewards of success!

TODAY

There are two days in every week that you should neither worry about nor fear. One of these days is yesterday, with its mistakes, its aches and pains, its faults and blunders. Yesterday has passed forever beyond your control. All the money in the world cannot bring back yesterday. You cannot erase a single word—yesterday is gone. The other day you should not worry about is tomorrow, with its large promise and possible burdens. Tomorrow is also beyond your immediate control. Tomorrow's sun will rise, either in splendor or behind a mask of clouds—but it will rise. You have no stake in tomorrow, because it hasn't arrived yet. This leaves only one day—today! Anybody can fight the battle of just one day. It is only when you take on the burdens of yesterday and tomorrow that you break down. Yesterday is history, tomorrow is a mystery, today is a gift—that is why they call it the present!

<u>PERSISTENCE</u>

In the quest for success, everyone must encounter the closed door marked "failure." Most people will stop dead in their tracks because they don't think they have the key to open it. But what they don't realize is that door is merely an obstacle they can unlock with the key of persistence. People who are successful never quit because their persistence won't let them. They realize that failure is merely a detour on the way to their goal. Calvin Coolidge once said, "Your ability to face setbacks and disappointments without giving up will be the measure of your ability to succeed." He was right. Most philosophers agree you can never simply fail. However, you can stop trying. Getting knocked down is no disgrace; staying there is.

DECISIONS

Life is a sequence of choices. The decisions you make today will create events in your life tomorrow. If you eat two slices of pecan pie every night, what is the inevitable outcome? If you smoke two packs of cigarettes daily, what is the inevitable eventuality? Everything you are presently doing will affect your present or your future. The choice is yours. You will make many decisions today. Some of them will give you pleasure now, but tomorrow you will be miserable over those decisions. Some of those decisions may make you a little uncomfortable today, but, tomorrow, you will be thrilled. Reprogram your thinking to distance. Reprogram your life for endurance. Patience is powerful. Your decisions today can create the circumstances you desire tomorrow.

HEALTH

Many mental factors are involved in being happy and successful. Having a positive attitude, being persistent and setting goals are just a few. However, there is a physical element that is also involved in being happy and successful, and that is your health. The great thing about your health is that you can control it with the habits you keep. You decide whether to exercise or not, whether to eat properly or not. In a study of 7,000 people in Alameda County, California, researchers found that the healthiest people develop 7 basic habits: They don't smoke cigarettes, they have regular physical activity, they use alcohol moderately or never, they get 7 to 8 hours of sleep every night, they maintain their proper weight, they eat breakfast and they avoid eating between meals. And remember, a healthy body leads to a healthier mind!

LISTENING

An 89-year-old woman had a hearing problem. Her doctor said, "We have a procedure that can correct your hearing. When would you like me to schedule it?" She said, "Forget it, I'm 89 and I've already heard enough." Most of us have not heard enough. We need our hearing corrected. The biggest problem in marriages today is communication. Not just talking, but listening. Most sales people lose sales because they are too busy speaking instead of listening to their customers. If you are fortunate, when you are born you can see, but you have to learn to read. And if you're fortunate, when you are born you can hear, but you must learn to listen. The average person can speak 180 words per minute, but can hear up to 500 words per minute. So, focus on the person you're with. Listen to others the way you want others to listen to you.

<u>CLASS</u>

When others speak well of you, you've got acceptance. But when the truth speaks well about you, you've got class! Class is just confidence dressed in humility. It keeps its word, its temper and its friends. It has a steady eye, a steady tongue and steady habits. It's silent when it has nothing to say, thoughtful when it judges. It's always first to make amends when it's wrong. Class has a sense of humor. It knows how to laugh. Class never makes excuses. It takes its lumps, learns from its mistakes and becomes wiser. Class knows that courtesy and good manners are nothing more than a series of small sacrifices. Class can walk with kings, yet still keep its virtue, talk with crowds, yet maintain the common touch. Above all, everyone is comfortable with a person who has class, because they are comfortable with themselves!

TODAY

How are you living right now? Are you enjoying today? Read these words carefully. Just for today, I'll experience and enjoy each hour to the fullest and not try to tackle my whole life's problems at once. Just for today, I'll try to improve my mind by learning more. I'll read something that requires effort, thought and commitment. Just for today, I'll look my best, speak well and be considerate of others. Just for today, I won't find fault or try to change or improve anyone but myself. Just for today, I'll have a plan and a goal. I might not follow them exactly, but I'll have them nonetheless. By doing this, I'll save myself from two enemies—hurry and indecision. Just for today, I'll exercise my character. I'll do something good for someone and keep it a secret. Just for today, I won't be afraid to love or to risk. Just for today, take a good look around you and be thankful you live in America today.

GRATITUDE

Do you have an attitude of gratitude or are you a constant complainer? Here is a morning prayer you should remember: "Even though I clutch my blanket and growl when the alarm goes off, thank you that I can hear—there are many who are deaf. Even though I close my eyes as long as possible against the morning light, thank you that I can see—there are many who are blind. Even though I huddle in my bed and put off the effort to rise, thank you that I have the strength to get up—there are many who are bedridden. Even though the first hour of my day is hectic, when socks are lost, toast is burned and tempers are short, thank you for my family—there are many who are all alone. Even though our breakfast never looks like the pictures in the magazines and the menu at times is limited, thank you for the food we have—there are many who are hungry. Count your blessings every day, for there are many who won't make it through the day.

LIFE

In his essay "The Station," Robert Hastings writes, "Tucked away in our subconscious, we see ourselves on a long train trip that spans the continent. As we look out the windows, we drink in the passing scenes—children waving, cattle grazing, city skylines and village halls. But uppermost in our minds is the final destination. On a certain day, we'll pull into the station, bands will play, and flags will wave. Once we arrive, we believe, so many wonderful dreams will come true. Restlessly we pace the aisles, despising the minutes, waiting for that station. When we reach the station, that will be it, we cry! When I buy my Mercedes. When I get married. When I've paid off the mortgage. When I retire. Waiting for the station. But sooner or later we realize that the true joy of life is not the destination, but the journey itself." So stop pacing the aisles and counting the miles. Enjoy the journey. The station will come soon enough.

<u>GROWING</u>

By the time most people are in their mid-30s, they've
stopped acquiring any new skills or new attitudes. Does
that surprise you? How long has it been since you
acquired a new skill? How many new attitudes have you
adopted lately? At work? At home? In your spiritual
journey? With your personal finances? Are you stuck in
a rut? Do you feel compelled to approach a problem the
same way every time? Does a new idea make you put
up your guard? Are you addicted to predictability?
When was the last time you did something for the first
time? Most people agree that growing is a good thing,
yet few dedicate themselves to the process. Living and
learning go hand in hand—just like living and breathing.
The same hours and minutes that capture the wonder of
a child can deepen the rut of an adult. The best way
to keep from becoming complacent and continuing to
grow is to make learning a lifetime commitment!

CHALLENGES

No matter who you are, "challenges" are just part of life. Think about this for a moment: the salesman has his quotas; the performer has his rehearsals; the pilot has to stay strapped in for hours; the minister is never free from sermon preparation. How about the truck driver who deals with the daily grind of traffic, weather hazards and monotonous miles? Then there's the mother with tiny children, facing 14 hours a day of making decisions, competing with strong wills and trying to be everything to everybody. Everyone has been given an assignment that comes with a challenge. The poet said, "I grumbled that I had no shoes, till I met a man who had no feet." It's all about attitude. And with the right perspective and attitude you can overcome any challenge in your life.

LISTENING

Current studies show that most people forget 50 percent of what they hear immediately, 80 percent within 24 hours, and 97 percent within a week. How can you become a better listener? When you listen, make your goal understanding—not just remembering the facts. Great learners are great listeners. That is why they always have a fresh flow of ideas, concepts and insights. Here are three tips to help you become a better listener: Look at the speaker—focus on him; Don't interrupt—let the speaker finish his thoughts and sentences; and don't judge—wait to hear the whole story before you respond. If you don't, you may miss the most important thing the speaker has to say. Here's a reminder: the reason God gave you two ears and one mouth is so that you would listen twice as much as you speak!

PERSEVERANCE

Thomas Edison once said, "Many of life's failures are men who did not realize how close they were to success when they gave up." Walt Disney was actually fired by a newspaper editor who told him, "You're not creative enough!" Richard Bach wrote a story about a seagull and was turned down by 18 different publishers. Undeterred, he kept knocking on doors until finally McMillan published his story. Within five years, "Jonathan Livingston Seagull" had sold more than 7 million copies. Don't ever give up! Perseverance is the power to endure and face defeat without giving up. Successful people realize that rejection or defeat is merely a temporary setback on the way to their goal or dream. The key to persevering is to feed your faith and starve your fear. Both of them will be with you, but the one you act upon will dominate your life. Remember, success and victory go to the people who never give in, never give up and never quit!

OVERCOMING FAILURE

As you drive toward your destiny, you'll hit some potholes and occasionally take a few wrong turns. Actually, the only way to avoid failure is to never leave your driveway! The issue is not whether you are going to fail, but whether you're going to learn from it and make it an asset. Are you going to turn it into wisdom to succeed and move forward? In a recent survey of highly successful people, none of them viewed their mistakes as failures. They simply called them "learning experiences," "tuition paid" or "opportunities for growth." The next time you fail at something, ask yourself these questions: "What have I learned?" "How can I turn it into success?" "Where do I go from here?" "How can my experience help others?" "Did I actually fail, or did I just fall short of an unrealistically high goal?" Failure is success if you learn from it!

POSITIVE ATTITUDE I

What does it mean to have a great attitude? You've probably heard the old expression that a positive person sees a glass half full instead of half empty. That's true, but only a small part of the story. Positive people see the best in others; they see opportunity everywhere; they focus on solutions; they are persistent, generous people; they are big givers; and they take responsibility for their lives. Do you? Unsuccessful people avoid responsibility, but a successful person understands that nothing positive happens until you're willing to step forward and take full responsibility for your thoughts and actions. What you believe about life determines how you perceive life, which determines what you receive in life. Your attitude toward life determines life's attitude toward you.

POSITIVE ATTITUDE II

Your mind is a thought factory that produces thousands of thoughts each day. Your factory is controlled by one of two foremen—Mr. Positive Attitude or Mr. Negative Attitude. Mr. Positive specializes in producing reasons why you can handle whatever comes your way, why you're more than able to conquer, why you can win and succeed. Mr. Negative, on the other hand, is an expert in producing reasons why you can't succeed and why you should give up. Both foremen are instantly obedient; they snap to attention when you give the signal. That is why you need to send the right educational and informational signals. As soon as Mr. Positive receives them, he turns on the switch and sends one encouraging thought after another. But turn Mr. Negative loose, and he'll convince you why you can't, won't and shouldn't. Always have and maintain a positive attitude—you have to deposit the right thoughts into your memory bank!

GOALS

One of the major causes of failure is the unwillingness to take time to set goals. Goals are the alpha and omega of success, the beginning and the end. Goals create your road map for achievement. Most people have heard about goals, yet few practice this powerful discipline. Goal setting takes time, discipline, courage and patience. Why should you make goal-setting a lifetime habit? Goals give you a sense of purpose, something concrete to focus on. That focus will positively impact your actions. The future doesn't get better by hoping; it gets better but by having a plan. Which did you plan for more, your wedding or your marriage? Which do you plan for more, your vacation or your life? No one ever accomplishes anything worthwhile without a goal. Above all, keep in mind that the most important thing about goals is making some!

GROWTH

Poet Robert Browning wrote, "Why do we stay on the earth except to grow?" Most people would agree that growing is a good thing, but relatively few people dedicate themselves to the process. Why? Because growth requires change, and most people are reluctant to change. The truth is that without change, growth is impossible. Growth demands a temporary surrender of security, getting out of your comfort zone. It may mean giving up familiar but limiting patterns, safe but unrewarding work, values no longer believed in, relationships that have lost their meaning. Most people do not realize that successful and unsuccessful people do not differ substantially in their abilities. The difference is in their desire to reach their potential. Nothing is more effective when it comes to reaching your potential than a commitment to personal growth!

WORDS

Your tongue is one of the most powerful gifts ever placed at your command. Life and death are in the power of the tongue. So often we do not think before we speak or consider the effect our words will have. Words like "I can't do that," "I can't handle it" or "This will never change" don't just affect those around you—they also infect you! Words have power because they create your world. More than anything that anyone else says, you believe what comes out of your own mouth. Refuse to release words of defeat, depression and discouragement. Your words are life! By thinking and speaking positively, you open the doors to make your optimism come true. Your words have the ability to build or destroy. Make sure you use them wisely!

GROWING

A teacher with 25 years of experience and a new college graduate both applied for the same job. When the new graduate got the job, the experienced teacher demanded to know why. The superintendent said, "It may be true that you have 25 years' experience, but after checking your record, I discovered that you only taught for one year and repeated it for the next 24!" It is not how much time you put in—it's what you put into the time that counts. Everybody has experiences; the difference is some go through them and others grow through them. You must grow and learn every day. Don't stop growing and don't just recycle what you learned years ago. Your mind is the drawing board for tomorrow's circumstances. You will never be promoted until you become overqualified for your present position.

SELF-EVALUATION

Did you hear about the guy named Bill who phoned his boss, disguised his voice and said, "I hear you're looking for a sharp, honest, hard-working young man." The boss replied, "Sorry, we already have someone like that. By the way, what's your name? Laughing, Bill replied, "This is Bill—and I was just checking up on myself!" When's the last time you checked up on yourself to see what kind of job you're doing? Are you diligent? Thoughtful? Loyal? Skillful? Teachable? Thorough? Fair? Honest? Cooperative? Positive? In today's world, the market- place rewards those whose eyes are on the task, not the clock; it rewards people who think, "Why not," instead of, "Why me?" Remember, you can either endure or enjoy your job, but understand this—the place you work will never be any better than you make it!

PATIENCE

Some of your greatest mistakes will happen because of impatience. Patience is not just the ability to wait; it's the ability to keep a good attitude while you're waiting. In 1879, a man called Pearl Wait invented Jell-O. He tried selling it door-to-door with other homemade remedies that he had invented, but when sales weren't strong, he sold his rights for $450 to a man called Woodward. Woodward knew the value of marketing and long-term planning, and within eight years, he had turned Jell-O into a million-dollar business. Today, not one of Pearl Wait's relatives receives a penny in royalties from the 1.1 million boxes of Jell-O that are sold daily. Why? Because Pearl Wait couldn't wait! Life is a marathon, not a 50-yard dash. Learn to pace yourself!

HOPE

A boy named Tommy had a particularly hard time in school. He constantly asked questions and was never able to keep up with the other kids in his class. His teacher finally gave up on him and told his mother that he couldn't learn and would never amount to much. But Tommy's mother was a nurturer; she believed in him. She taught him at home, and each time he failed, she gave him hope and encouraged him to keep trying. Whatever happened to Tommy? Well, eventually he grew up and became an inventor with more than 1,000 patents, including the phonograph and the first electric light bulb. His full name was Thomas Edison. Your words have power, so use every opportunity to teach faith, confidence, life and hope to other people. When people have hope and encouragement, there's no telling how far they can go!

<u>HABITS</u>

You have probably heard the saying, "The quality of preparation determines the quality of performance." A great concert pianist invests hundreds of hours of practice before his concert. He knows that the quality of those many grueling hours of practice will prepare him for his greatest performance. The heavyweight boxing champion of the world knows it would be too late to wait until he gets into the ring with his opponent to prepare. So for months before the fight, he toils by working out, running and exercising daily. Champions are only recognized in the ring. They become champions because of their daily routine. The secret of your future is hidden in your daily routine. The secret of your marriage, sales, health and business are all hidden in your daily routine. Remember, your habits today will determine what you have and become tomorrow.

IDEAS

Author Victor Hugo once said, "There's nothing more powerful than an idea whose time has come." Ideas are the greatest resource a successful person could ever have. And when you surround yourself with creative people, you're never at a loss for inspiring ideas. If you continually have good ideas, you have a better opportunity to reach your potential. How do you come up with ideas? Through believing you are capable of creative thinking. Most people use only a fraction of their brainpower and simply don't trust the rest. You are capable of generating good ideas—probably more than you think. First, realize that the only bad ideas are those that die without giving rise to other ideas. Second, realize that great ideas are often nothing more than the restructuring of what you already know.

<u>FRIENDSHIPS</u>

Charles "Tremendous" Jones said that the only difference between the person you are today and the person you will be in five years will come from the books you read and the people you associate with. Every day you choose who your closest friends are and who you hang out with. If you choose negative friends, you are also choosing a negative attitude, which will eventually turn into a negative life. But when you spend time with positive people, you help yourself to see things in a better light and position yourself to win and succeed in life. Your best friends will always be those who bring out the best in you. Think about what your friends bring out in you, and if it's not your best, it might be time to make some changes. Here's an easy reminder: people are like elevators. They can bring you up or take you down.

HAPPINESS

Happiness is basically feeling good about yourself. Don't confuse happiness with popularity, which means that others feel good about you. What you think about yourself, your character and your own accomplishments determines your real sense of worth and value. There are two elements vital to your happiness—your relationships and your achievements. Life was never meant to be an endurance of trials, but an enjoyment of triumphs and accomplishments. And the best part of life, particularly if you live in America, is that you get to decide! Too many people look to someone else to bring them happiness. They are looking for material things and external solutions to an internal problem. Happiness does not start around you. It begins inside you!

ENTHUSIASM

Enthusiasm is an essential element if you are to have success. Enthusiasm is a zeal; it is fire and passion inside you. Enthusiasm separates those who just want to be successful from those who are successful. It will transform your life, because it produces energy. If you are excited about something, you are more likely to work harder to attain it. Enthusiasm is like adrenaline, pushing you to accomplish more with greater efficiency. Enthusiasm takes commitment, and commitment takes work. You are not going to get out of bed fired up every day, but it is up to you to change your attitude to a positive one. After all, what use is negative energy? It drains you of your most precious resource—your enthusiasm.

VISUALIZATION

Most people don't know what they want in life—what they want to be, where they want to go, what they want to see, share or do. Where are you headed? How are you going to get there? It doesn't matter where you started or where you are today. What matters is what you are doing right now. Too many people let life happen to them. Only a few decide for themselves what is going to happen to them. To just stay alive is not enough. You must have a picture of your life, because you can only do something you see. That's why people put pictures of a thin person on the refrigerator when they are trying to lose weight. It gives them a picture of what they want to be. When your heart decides on a destination, your mind will design a map to get there. While you can't decide when or how you are going to die, you can picture how you want to live!

ENTHUSIASM

Enthusiasm fuels your dream. Anything that you neglect will deteriorate. It could be your body, your marriage or the dream of your life. Enthusiasm will give you and those around you the energy, drive and encouragement to stay focused. What are you dreaming about today? What do you long to finish or achieve? Here are three keys to help you release the power of enthusiasm around you. 1) Create a visual representation or written goal and place it on the wall so you can look at it every day. Before and while I wrote my first book, I looked at the title every day. 2) Find people who believe in you and your dreams, people who will encourage and support you. 3) Realize that you are responsible for maintaining your own enthusiasm and the energy for achieving your dreams. It's not the responsibility of your spouse or boss. Remind yourself to take daily steps to create the climate of continuous victory in your life!

PASSION

If you're going to have long-term success in your career, you must pursue your passion, not your pension. When you pursue your passion, you'll be inspired to learn as much as you can and to gain as many skills as you can, and then you'll be sought after for your quality service and dedication to excellence. Your passion will make you oblivious to quitting time and to the length of your workday. You'll wake up every morning with the passion of pursuit, but not with the pursuit of money. Those who do more than they're paid for are always sought out for their services. Their passion qualifies them for promotion and financial rewards. Their name and work outlive them. If what you love begins to consume your mind, your thoughts, your conversations, your schedule, get ready for extraordinary success and results. You that you will only have significant success with something that you have passion for!

ADVERSITY

J.C. Penney once said, "I would have never amounted to anything were it not for adversity. I was forced to come up the hard way." Most people don't handle adversity very well, because they don't understand its advantages. What happens in life, happens to all of us. Whether you're black, white, Hispanic, Chinese, male, female, rich, poor, young or old, adversity is not prejudiced. It visits us all. Adversity is part of life, so let me help you change your thinking about it. Recognize that adversity will force you to dig for more accurate information and to pause for introspection. What lessons are you learning? What did you learn from this experience? Adversity reveals the depth of friendships. Who are your real friends? Adversity also strengthens you and helps you decide what you really believe. Remember, it's not what happens to you that matters, it's what you do with what happens to you that counts!

THE MIND

Every problem is a mind problem. So many people in the world have many more problems and challenges than you do today, yet but they still succeed and prosper, whether their problems are physical or emotional. Why? Because they have come to understand that the only barrier between them and anything they desire is the way they think. Your mind is the control mechanism of your entire life. It is a magnificent tool, and when you know how to use it, it will be a powerful tool to help you become and accomplish what you want. For instance, when you misspell a word on paper, where does the error come from—from the pencil, your hand, your fingers or the paper? None of these. The error comes from your mind. In the same way, a rewarding career, fulfilling relationships, wisdom, good health and wealth all begin in your mind before they manifest in your outer world. When you change your way of thinking, you will change your life forever!

RELATIONSHIPS

Napoleon conquered the world, yet when he died in exile on the island of St. Helena, he was alone and forsaken by all who knew him best. His wife went back to her father. His best friend deserted him without even saying goodbye. Two of his most trusted marshals openly insulted him, and even his faithful servants who slept outside his bedroom door left him. Why? Because he was self-centered! The people around him felt used but never appreciated. What a lesson—especially for people who think "they don't need others" or "they don't have time to waste on people." If you reach all your goals, but lose the people who matter the most in the process, what have you gained? Imagine having a story to tell, but nobody to listen, something to celebrate, but nobody to celebrate with. Don't let it happen to you. What you deposit into your relationships today is ALL you'll have to draw on later.

<u>EXCELLENCE</u>

An elderly carpenter was ready to retire, so he told his employer of his plans to leave the house-building business. The contractor was sorry to see one of the best workers go and asked if he could build one more house as a favor. The carpenter agreed, but it was easy to see that his heart was not in his work. He cut corners and used inferior materials. It was an unfortunate way to end his career. When the house was finished, the contractor came to inspect it and handed the front door key to the carpenter. "This is my gift to you," he said. "It is your house."

What a shock! What a shame! If only the carpenter had known he was building his own house, he would have done it all so differently. Remember that you are the carpenter of your life. Each day you hammer a nail, place a board or erect a wall. Build wisely. It is the only life you will ever build! Give it your best.

INTEGRITY

The difference between a leader and a manipulator is character. People are looking for leaders they can trust, leaders with integrity. Integrity is crucial for business and personal success. A joint study conducted by the UCLA Graduate School of Management and Korn/Ferry International of New York City surveyed 1,300 senior executives. Seventy-one percent said that integrity was the quality most needed to succeed in business. Another study by the Center for Creative Research found that though many errors and obstacles can be overcome by a person who wants to rise to the top of an organization, that person is almost never able to move up in the company if he or she compromises his or her integrity by betraying others' trust. Bear in mind that your integrity will be remembered much longer than your product, potential or productivity.

<u>WORDS</u>

The English language has more than 450,000 words. Yet the average daily conversations are made up of a mere 400 words—of which the most commonly used are I, ME, MY and MINE. One of the most important qualities of successful leaders is an ability to express thoughts and knowledge, to communicate effectively. Research by management and human resource experts confirms that no matter what field of employment, people with large vocabularies—those able to speak clearly and concisely, using simple as well as descriptive words—are the best at accomplishing their goals. Well-chosen words can close the sale, negotiate the raise, enhance relationships and change destinies. Words are the bridge to your future. Success is conceived in your mind, but your words give it life!

<u>LEGACIES</u>

Years ago, a sociological study asked 50 people over the age of 95 this question: "If you could live your life over again, what would you do differently?" It was an open-ended question with several responses. However, three answers constantly emerged and dominated the results of the study: 1) If I had it to do over again, I would reflect more, 2) If I had it to do over again, I would risk more, and 3) If I had it to do over again, I would do more things that would live on after I've died. Every day you have a chance to make a positive impact on your co-workers and customers. You can leave a heritage to your children that will last them a lifetime. You can leave a legacy in your company, industry and community. Make a commitment today. Make your life count!

GOALS

Did you know 50 percent of the people you know don't know where they're going? Another 40 percent will go in any direction they're led. The remaining 10 percent know where they would like to go, but fewer than half of them will ever pay the price to get there. The great J.C. Penney once said, "Give me a stock clerk with a goal, and I'll give you a man who'll make history. On the other hand, give me a man without a goal, and I'll give you a stock clerk." While you work on your goals, your goals are working on you. What you get by reaching them is not nearly as important as what you become on the way. What are your goals today? Are they clear enough to write down? Strong enough to help you persevere? Valuable enough to make you pay the price? Remember, winners make goals, losers make excuses!

ABILITY

All people are created with the equal ability to become unequal. Not everyone is equipped with the same talents, gifts and abilities; however, each one of us is created in a unique way. Personalities are as diverse as the universe itself. There is one constant: you can, by using what you have to the fullest, stand out from the crowd. Thomas Edison was almost deaf, but he didn't spend his time attempting to learn how to hear. Instead he focused on his ability to think, organize and create. His accomplishments speak well for his decision to build on the qualities he possessed. He took the ability inside of him and made the best of it. Your responsibility is to take the talents/abilities you've been given and develop them to the highest level possible!

COMMUNICATION

The words you use on a daily basis often determine the success and failure of your interactions with your spouse, co-workers or clients. According to research psychologists, the average one-year-old child has a three-word vocabulary. By 15 months of age, children can speak 19 words. At two years of age, most young-sters possess a working knowledge of 272 words. Their vocabulary catapults to 896 words by the age of three, 1,540 by age four and 2,072 words by age five. By age six, the average child can communicate with 2,562 words. Our word accumulation continues to grow, yet using the words effectively does not necessarily follow. When communicating, say what you mean and mean what you say!

PERSEVERANCE

Many people give up just when they're about to attain success. A high school basketball coach was attempting to motivate his players to persevere through a difficult season. Halfway through the season, he stood before his team and said, "Did Michael Jordan ever quit?" The team responded "No!" He yelled, "What about the Wright Brothers? Did they ever give up? "No!" the team resounded. "Did John Elway ever quit?" Again the team yelled, "No!" "Did Elmer McAllister ever quit?" There was a long silence. Finally, one player was bold enough to ask, "Who's Elmer McAllister? We've never heard of him." The coach snapped back, "Of course you've never heard of him—he quit!" Remember, when you want something you've never had, you have got to do something you've never done. Never give up!

<u>TIME</u>

The Great Benjamin Franklin once said, "If we take care of the minutes, the years will take care of themselves." One minute. It doesn't seem like much. However, if you were to place a one-dollar value on every minute of your life, in one year, you would have $525,600. Are you spending or investing your minutes? Time is a fixed income, and as with any income, the real challenge facing you is how to work successfully with your daily allotment. Plan each day down to the minute, because once you have wasted time, you can never get it back. The value you place on each minute of every day will determine the results you get in your life. Don't count the minutes, but make every minute count!

ATTITUDE

Harvard psychologist William James said, "The greatest discovery of my generation is that a human being can alter his life by altering his attitudes of the mind." Can our lives actually be enhanced by changing our attitudes? You bet! Whether you like it or not, who you become on the outside is who you are in the inside. Attitude is the reflection of a person and your world mirrors your attitude. Author James Allen put it this way: "A person cannot travel within and stand still without." Ultimately, what you experience, achieve or don't achieve depends on your attitude. Few things can stop the person with the right attitude, but nothing can help the one with the wrong attitude. What happens in life happens to all of us. It's not what happens to you that matters. It's what you do with what happens to you that counts!

MOTIVATION

Do you feel bored, unstimulated and unmotivated? Why? Life isn't boring, work isn't meaningless and relationships aren't valueless. The fact is, people can be boring, unexcited and unmotivated. They take their boredom from job to job, hoping that a new job, new people and a new environment will bring them out of the doldrums. It rarely works that way, and these people usually infect everyone around them. A motivated lifestyle is enjoyed by those who create it for themselves, whether it's through reading books, listening to a speaker or going to seminars. Motivation is like bathing—it is something you should do on a regular basis. It's your responsibility to generate your own motivation every day, with or without the assistance of others!

<u>PERSEVERANCE</u>

If you are facing obstacles on your quest for success, or you are coming up against some adversity in pursuit of your goals, understand that you must keep the faith and keep fighting, no matter what. You must persevere! How do you know when you have persevered enough? When you have achieved what you set out to do! In 1905, the University of Bern rejected a Ph.D. dissertation as irrelevant. Albert Einstein was disappointed, but not defeated. He persevered. Michael Jordan was cut from his high school basketball team. Henry Ford went bankrupt twice in his first three years in business. During its first year in business, the Coca-Cola Company sold only 400 Cokes. A football player was told he was too small and too weak to play football. Today, Fran Tarkenton is in the Hall of Fame. You may never make history, become a famous athlete or invent a new product, but whatever your dreams are, never quit!

STRESS

When was the last time you woke up refreshed, refueled and ready for the day? How long did you stay energized and excited about the day's activities? For too many people, the stress of life zaps their ability to do their best, be their best and enjoy their daily activities. Over 1 million Americans have heart attacks each year; 8 million have stomach ulcers. We have more than 12 million alcoholics in this country. These are just the tip of the iceberg of stress-related statistics. Stress is the wear and tear on your body caused by life's events. It's the body's physical, mental and chemical reactions to circumstances in your life. Most people take better care of their cars than they do of themselves. Learn to relax; it's cheaper than therapy. Take a recess; exercise, which will rejuvenate your system; and recognize your limits. If you adapt and create good habits you'll be on your way toward a healthy lifestyle.

WORK

In a national survey of 180,000 American workers, 80 percent indicated a dislike for their jobs. It's a sad reflection on an activity that will absorb a major portion of our lives. To make matters worse, people who dislike their vocation will never qualify for promotion or financial rewards. Think about Thomas Edison's perspective on work. He said, "I never did a day's work in my life. It was all fun." He believed the purpose of work was joy and fulfillment. So how do you get beyond the feeling that your work is only enjoyable at lunch time and on payday? To start with, study what you are doing, like what you are doing and believe in what you are doing! Stop looking at work simply as a means of earning a living and start realizing it is one of the keys to making a life.

<u>COMMITMENT</u>

Leaders, inventors, businesspeople, dreamers, aspiring professionals and anyone else desiring to achieve and succeed in their endeavors must understand that the first step is to make a commitment to invest their life and talents toward all pursuits deserving their best efforts. What you commit yourself to be will change who you are and make you into a different person. What are your commitments today? Where are you going? Who are you committed to? What are you going to be? Show me a person who hasn't decided, and I'll show you someone who has no identity, no personality and no direction. Remember, a total commitment is paramount to reaching your ultimate goal! Make a commitment today!

GROWTH

Did you hear about the frog who has hopping along one day, when he happened to slip into a large pothole? All his attempts to jump out, fell short. Soon a cat came upon the frog trapped in the hole and offered to pull him out. He too failed. Several other animals tried to help the poor frog, but they all gave up. "We'll go back and get you some food," they said. "It looks like you're going to be there a while." However, not long after they took off to get food, the frog hopped past them. They couldn't believe it! "We thought you couldn't get out of there," they hollered. "Oh, I couldn't," replied the frog, " but you see, there was a big tractor coming right at me and I had to." That's how it is with many people. Only when they have to get out of potholes and the ruts of life do they make changes. Consider the advice of Mark Twain, who said, "Take your mind out every now and then and dance on it. It is getting all caked up." He knew people have a tendency to get in a rut easily. Don't let it happen to you!

<u>READING</u>

Fifty percent of Americans don't read books. Yet studies show that high-income people read an average of 19 books per year. It's been said that the person who can read and doesn't, has no advantage over the person who can't read. If you would commit to read one nonfiction book a month—12 books a year—you would be in the top 1 percent in the nation. Do you think—when most people aren't even trying to acquire more information or knowledge—you would have an edge? You bet! However, that's just a start. It's not what or how many books you read that counts, it's what you apply that ensures your growth. Reading is not a leisure luxury but a life-enhancing necessity if you are to attain your goals!

<u>EXAMPLE</u>

A blind man in the city was sitting at a street corner with a lantern beside him. A woman passed by, noticed the man and inquired why he had a lantern even though he was blind. The blind man simply replied, "So that no one may stumble over me." He was holding a lantern so others would see him. As a leader or manager in your organization, is your behavior, or are your actions, the example of the behavior you expect from your employees? Leaders in any organization must model the behavior they desire from the rest of the company or team. Whether you're a company executive, teacher, spouse, minister, little league baseball coach, big league player or political leader, the message is the same. Let your lantern burn brightly so others won't stumble. People may doubt what you say, but they will believe what you do!

FOCUS

One of the primary reasons organizations and people don't reach the levels of success they desire is because their focus is broken. Focus is anything that consumes your time, energy, finances and attention. If you are going to have success in your career, marriage, health or any area of your life, you're going to have to decide and define what you want and then focus! Your focus determines your energy. It determines your mastery and your future. Fragmented or broken focus, on the other hand, destroys your dream. It creates an unending parade of tragedies and disasters in your life. For example, bad friendships—they do not feed, fuel or fertilize your focus on your goals. Get rid of them. Be the gatekeeper of your eyes, ears and heart. In order to live your dreams, you have to unclutter your life and get rid of distractions so you can focus!

ATTITUDE

Yogi Berra once said, "Life is like baseball; it's 95 percent mental and the other half is physical." Despite his math, Berra knew how much the average person underestimates the role of the mind in the success process. If you have intelligence, talent, education, technical know-how, opportunities and a strong work ethic, yet lack the right attitude, you are severely limiting your ability to succeed and to enjoy the journey of life. Having a good attitude makes all the difference in the world. When you were born, everything was out of your control. You couldn't choose your parents, where you were born or any of the circumstances. But today, if you're over 18, you're completely responsible for your choices and your attitude. Your life is not determined by what happens to you, but by the attitude you bring to life!

<u>GIVING</u>

Are you a giver or a taker? Nothing has as much of a positive impact on people as giving to others. People who have a giving spirit are some of the most positive people on earth, because giving is the highest form of living. These people focus their time and energy on what they can give to others rather than what they can get from them. And studies show that the more they give, the better their attitude. Most unsuccessful people don't understand this concept. They think that the amount people give and their attitude are based on how much they have. But that's not true. The fact is, there are plenty of people who have been blessed with money, good families and great careers who are greedy, stingy and suspicious of others. Remember, it's not what you have that makes a difference; it's what you do with what you have. And that is based on your attitude!

THOUGHTS

We have all heard the old adage, "You are what you think," but the truth is, your thought condition will influence your life condition. Many people hurt their chance for success by sabotaging themselves with negative thought patterns, not understanding that those thought patterns will ultimately influence their behavior. One of the major influences of your thought condition is the people surrounding you. Negative thinkers tend to surround themselves with negative and discouraging people. They feel comfortable in these surroundings, because they don't have to live up to anyone's expectations, and, therefore, they have an excuse to fail. These people are dangerous, because their views are contagious and erode self-esteem. Do you surround yourself with people who believe in you and lift your spirits? Or do you spend time with people who bring you down? Surround yourself with positive thoughts and positive people every day!

WINNERS

It's pretty simple to tell a winner from a loser. A winner says, "Let's find out"; a loser says, "Nobody knows." When a winner makes a mistake, he says, "I was wrong"; when a loser makes a mistake, he says, "It wasn't my fault." A winner makes commitments; a loser makes only promises. A winner goes through a problem; a loser goes around it, and never gets past it. A winner says, "I'm good, but not as good as I ought to be"; a loser says, "I'm not as bad as a lot of other people." A winner respects those who are superior to him and tries to learn something from them; a loser resents those who are superior to him and tries to find kinks in their armor. A winner feels responsible for more than his job; a loser says, "I only work here." A winner doesn't care who gets the credit; a loser takes all the credit but passes blame. If you want to be a winner, think like a winner, act like a winner, and sooner than you think, you will be a winner!

POTENTIAL

There isn't a ruler, yardstick or measuring tape in the world large enough to compute the strength and capabilities of the giant who is fast asleep within you. Its size and power are unlimited. Its force is that of a million dynamos. Its tireless energy is beyond all comprehension. It's the giant of your untapped potential; it's your ability to unfold, to develop and to grow. It will continue to lie there peacefully asleep until you decide to wake it. Like the desert lacking water, too often people endure shortages in their lives, when all they have to do is simply open the valves—the valves of attitudes, habits, focus and a plan of action to achieve what is lacking. The giant who sleeps in all people only awakens when they take control of their abilities, talent and skills. They tap their potential by taking action in a personal way. So can you.

ENCOURAGEMENT

Encouragement is the seed of inspiration. In the early 19th century, a young man in London aspired to be a writer. But everything seemed to be against him. He had not been able to attend school for more than four years. His father had been thrown into jail, and he often knew the pangs of hunger. He got a job in a rat-infested warehouse, and he slept in the slums. He had so little confidence in his writing abilities that he mailed his first manuscript in the dead of the night so nobody would laugh at him. Story after story was refused. One day, one story was finally accepted. True, he wasn't paid a shilling, but one editor did praise him. One editor gave him recognition. Because of the praise, recognition and encouragement of just one person, this young boy was transformed into one of the most noted writers of all time. His name? Charles Dickens. You have the power to encourage, too. Whether it's a child, spouse or employee, nothing stimulates growth so much as praise and encouragement!

ENTHUSIASM

If you are in the habit of driving to work, dreading the day—consider this. Years ago Dr. Norman Vincent Peale wrote a book entitled "Enthusiasm Makes the Difference" in which he detailed a formula that may help you put every day in a positive perspective. The first step is to "Think a Good Day." If you have a positive image of the day before it unfolds, it will help you get going in the right direction. Second, "Thank a Good Day." Give thanks for a good day in advance and that positive imagery will help make it so. Third, "Plan a Good Day." Plan some positive things that you have control over into your day to help get it on the right track. Next, "Put Good in the Day." Put good thoughts, good attitudes and good actions into a day, and they will make the day good. Finally, fill the day with enthusiasm. Give the day all you've got and it will give right back to you. Our days are few, so make the best of them. Enthusiasm makes the difference!

CRITICS

Success is like a blackboard—when you make your mark on the world, watch out for the people with erasers! It really doesn't matter what profession you are in, you are going to meet and be confronted by critics. It has always amazed me that most critics generally have never walked a mile in the shoes of those they criticize, yet they still don't hesitate to pass harsh words. The fact is, critics are spectators, not players. Critical people are usually disheartened people who have failed to reach a desired goal. Someone once said, "Criticism is the death gargle of a non-achiever." Criticism points out your flaws, but correction points out your potential. There has never been a monument built to a critic. Be aware that the critics are out there. Don't let them hold you back or slow you down!

OBSTACLES

Earl Nightingale once said, "Before you begin anything worthwhile, obstacles will swarm to confront you. If you start counting the obstacles, you'll never stop counting them. However, once you start, you won't stop to count." No matter who you are, or where you're from, you are going to run into obstacles. So how do you overcome obstacles in your life? First, look at them not as obstacles but as hurdles you must jump over. Think of the hurdles as a challenge to win the race. That is what a woman named Mary Gord-Lewis did. She was born with dyslexia and because she came from a tough environment, she was a street fighter who got caught up in petty theft, alcohol and drugs. At the age of 16, Mary still couldn't read. She gave birth out of wedlock and raised two children on her own. But as Oliver Wendell Holmes said, "What lies behind us, what lies ahead of us, is of little importance when compared to what lies inside of us." Today, Mary's full name reads Mary Gord-Lewis M.D. Use your stumbling blocks as stepping stones to do something better today!

COMMUNICATION

Don't be so wrapped up in your own life that you forget how to relate to others. Lack of communication is one of the biggest problems you will encounter in life, whether it's your employees, your associates, your boss or even your family. True communication is more than just listening and speaking to someone. It is also being friendly and helpful. (Remember, if you want a friend, be one.) It is also smiling—it takes 72 muscles to frown, only 14 to smile—and it is being generous with praise and cautious with criticism. It is being genuinely interested in people. You can like almost everybody if you try. It is being alert to give service. What counts most in life is what we do for others. Have a good sense of humor, a big dose of patience and a dash of humility, and you'll be rewarded many-fold!

TEAMWORK

Someone once said, "Coming together is a beginning; keeping together is progress; working together is success." He was right. One day a father called his six sons together to teach them a lesson that would help them throughout their life. He had already gathered a bundle of six sticks, which he had carefully tied together with a string. One by one, he asked his six sons to take the bundle and break it. All six of them failed. Then the father took out a knife and cut the string and distributed a single stick to each of the six sons. He repeated the request that they break the single stick. This time, each son broke his stick. The father looked at them and said, "When you work together in a spirit of harmony, you resemble the bundle of sticks, and no one can defeat you, but when you quarrel among yourselves, anyone can defeat you one at a time." Remember, a house or team divided against itself cannot stand or win!

FEAR

The best way of overcoming fear is to take the word fear and break it down by its letters which actually stand for false evidence appearing real. When you think of fear in this context, it becomes easier to overcome. Bill Emmerton overcame fear in a big way. Bill, in his late 40s, had set a goal of running through Death Valley. Most people know about the torturing heat, but few know that the valley is 125 miles long. As Bill began his journey, the temperature was 106. He was soon met by a raging sand storm so severe that it picked him up off the ground and blew him 15 feet. But he refused to let fear stop him. Bill kept going. Later, the temperature escalated to 135 degrees and he had to finish with the toe of his shoe cut off to allow for the circulation of blood. Bill didn't let the fear of the heat or desert interfere with his goal—he finished the run. The fear of failure will never overtake you, if you remember that most fears are based on appearances, not reality.

PERSISTENCE

There may be no characteristic more important in obtaining success than persistence. That special trait is found in all winners, because it relentlessly drives them toward excellence. Persistence also enables winners to bounce back after defeat, and whip any negative thought that approaches their mind. The ability to be persistent is in all great success stories because along the way, successful people all faced obstacles that tested their persistence. Remember the words of the former heavy-weight boxing champion James Corbett who said, "Fight one more round. When your feet are so tired that you have to shuffle back to the center of the ring, fight one more round. When your arms are so tired that you can hardly lift your hands, fight one more round. When your nose is bleeding and your eyes are black, fight one more round, remembering that the man who always fights one more round is never whipped." Remember, success is getting up one more time than you fall!

GOALS

One of the major causes of failure is the unwillingness to take the time to set goals. However, there is more to goal setting than just sitting down and saying, "Hey, I want to do this." You must have a plan of action and a burning desire that will spark a total commitment. At the age of 15, John Goddard sat down and made a list of all the things he wanted to do in his lifetime. That list totaled 127: he wanted to write a book, run a five-minute mile, sail around the world, and take a boat up the Nile River. At the age of 26, Goddard was found at the beginning of the Nile River. The local government had warned him that his goal of making the 4,000-mile journey was impossible. During the trip, Goddard and his party met several obstacles, including a hippo attack, bouts with malaria, blinding sand storms and miles of dangerous rapids. But in the end, because of his determination, Goddard finally sailed into the Mediterranean Sea. By the age of 60, Goddard had met 105 of his 127 goals. Remember, obstacles are only those frightful things you see when you take your eyes off the goal!

<u>RESISTANCE</u>

In 1954, all the leading medical journals said that the four-minute mile was not humanly possible. Doctors warned athletes of the dire consequences of attempting it. Coaches encouraged their runners to do their best but forget about achieving it. However, that same year, Roger Bannister broke the four-minute mile! Forty years later, Eamonn Coghlan of Ireland did it too—at the age of 41. When you begin to believe that you can achieve your goal, you activate motivation, commitment, confidence, concentration and excitement inside of you. Henry Ford was right when he said, "Whether you think you can or you can't, either way you're right." Believing doesn't mean it's going to be easy. The path to personal achievement is uphill all the way. But whether it's athletics, business, sales or academics, keep in mind that airplanes and kites rise faster when they fly into the wind. Keep in mind that you only grow stronger when resistance and opposition tests you.

<u>SMILES</u>

Of all the things you put on in the morning, a smile is probably the most valuable. Don't just give your employees or associates instructions—smile while you're doing it. If your husband or wife works in a difficult environment, make sure he or she doesn't come home to more of the same. Smiles are like thermostats—they set the temperature and determine the climate around you. Joy is infectious. How people see you determines how they will treat you. Nobody wants to be around somebody who looks like they'll bite your head off at any moment. Learn to smile; it opens doors and hearts. It causes others to relax and to lower their guard. Smiling says, "I'm happy to be with you" to someone you know, and it says, "I'm glad to meet you" to someone you just met. Whether you wear a smile or have a positive attitude, the choice is yours alone!

COURAGE

Courage is much more than a feeling. Check the record—anybody who ever beat the odds did it in spite of their fear! They did it because they were inspired by somebody else's example or words, they were moved by a need, and they said to themselves, "If not me, who? If not now, when?" They didn't think much about it at all or they might have changed their mind. If you are waiting for a feeling of courage, forget about it because it doesn't exist! You're only courageous when you do what's right—despite your fear. And since all of us feel fear, every one of us is capable of acting courageously. It's a choice! Any time you go where you've never been or try something you've never done, fear will be present. It will always stand between you and anything worth doing. Courage is overcoming and mastering fear—not the absence of fear. The choice is yours!

OBSTACLES

You are as big as you think. If you don't believe that statement, then read this story of John and Greg Rice. These two twins were born as dwarfs. Shortly after birth, they were abandoned by their parents because the couple wouldn't accept the responsibility of raising a pair of clubfoot dwarfs. Nine months later a couple took them in. But while in grade school, both of the adults died. Still, the twins maintained an unbelievable, positive attitude and made a goal in high school that they would some day be millionaires. They started out as door-to-door salesmen and soon ended up owning the company and becoming the millionaires that they dreamed of as youngsters. John and Greg didn't let the obstacle of their physical abilities interfere with their will and drive to succeed. Remember, the difference between a successful person and others is not a lack of height, but rather a lack of will!

REST

A tired mind rarely makes good decisions. Fatigue can be very costly. Yet many people who are capable of managing companies and developing complex budgets don't have the sense to know when they need a break, or how to use their resources without depleting them. If you're wise, you won't just put appointments on your calendar, you'll schedule some "down time" too. Well-timed rest restores your energy and maintains your abilities, so that you can function at full capacity. Many people are like the driver who's so concerned about where he's going and how fast he can get there that he doesn't notice that the engine's knocking, the tires are losing air and the gas tank is almost empty. Then, when the car breaks down, he asks, "What happened?" Life is demanding. In fact, the more you succeed, the more people will demand of you, but it is up to you to rest and repair yourself. Work hard, but play just as enthusiastically!

TIMING AND PREPARATION

Have you heard about the Chinese bamboo tree? During the first four years of its life, it grows only a few inches. Then in the fifth year, it grows 90 feet in just five weeks. Now the real question is, did it grow 90 feet in five weeks or five years? The answer: five years. You see, if at any time during those first four years you'd stopped watering and fertilizing the tree, it would have died. Our lives are like that. They are lived on different levels and arrive in seasons. You stay on one level and learn its lessons until you become qualified to move to the next. Don't be impatient about your goals, dreams or success. We live in a world where many people just want instant money, instant success, instant fame, instant everything! They do not understand timing, preparation and perseverance. It takes time to know your business. It takes time to know your product. It takes time to develop relationships and loyal customers. Don't rush!

TEAMWORK

Of the 21 most notable civilizations in history, 19 died
or crumbled from within. Similarly, teams, organizations
and even families fail to meet their potential or never
find true happiness and success because they let petty
jealousies and minor differences interfere with their
common goal. One of the greatest dynasties the world
has ever known was the Roman Empire, which spanned
continents over centuries and seemed indestructible.
But, eventually, the Roman Empire did fall—and not
because of outside factors. The empire fell from feuding
within its own ranks. You see, an individual's commitment
to a group effort is what makes a team work, a company
work and a community work! Teamwork can conquer
adversity, but dissension from within can crumble even
the greatest of empires.

OPTIMISM

Abraham Lincoln said, "An optimist is one who sees opportunity in every difficulty. A pessimist is one who sees difficulty in every opportunity." He was right. Optimism is an attitude, an outlook and a perception all in one. There is an organization directed toward optimistic people, as well as toward pursuing change in a pessimistic society. The members have an international creed that is worth repeating: "Be so strong that nothing can disturb your peace of mind. Talk health, happiness and prosperity to every person you meet. Make all your friends feel there is something in them worthwhile. Look at the sunny side of everything and make your optimism come true." You see, adversity or difficulty can make you tender or tough, bitter or better—it all depends on you. Think only the best, work only for the best, do only your best and expect only the best!

TEAMWORK

Have you ever wondered why some teams and companies are so successful, but others crumble and never make it to the top? Bill Russell of the Boston Celtics, who won 11 NBA titles as a player and two as a coach, has been asked the same question. His response went something like this: "There were Jews, Catholics, Protestants on our team, white men and black men on our team. The one thing we shared in common was an Irish name. One of our secrets was that we never had any cliques. We simply considered ourselves a proud group of men who bore the distinction of being something no one else could be in our sport—the champions of the world." What drove them to excellence wasn't the color of their skin or the selfishness of their egos. In fact, they had nothing in common except the cause of the team. They simply looked at all their differences and blended them into their greatest strength. So if you want a great team, be a great teammate!

PERSISTENCE

The great Elbert Hubbard wrote, "There is no defeat, except in no longer trying; no really insurmountable barrier, save our own inherent weakness of purpose." You must have persistence to overcome the adversities you'll face today and tomorrow. Charles Lindbergh said it this way: "Success is not measured by what a man accomplishes, but by the opposition he encountered, and the courage he maintained in his struggle against it." The University of Chicago conducted a five-year survey of the 20 top performers in various fields, including musicians, athletes, sculptors, mathematicians, physicians, actors, artists, scholars and chief executives. They also interviewed the families and teachers of these celebrated high achievers to find out how they did it. They discovered that drive and determination, not talent, led to their success. Great works are performed not by strength, but by persistence!

<u>HONESTY</u>

Two paths lie before all of us: honesty and dishonesty. The shortsighted embark on the dishonest path, not realizing that liars are eventually exposed. It may take weeks or even months, but the truth always surfaces. If it's in your marriage, lies are like termites in a tree— it may survive for years, but inevitably it will fall, taking a lot of other things with it. If it's in your career, ask the student who was just expelled for cheating or the worker who was fired for embezzling if it was worth it. Dishonesty always destroys trust, peace of mind and credibility. The wise embark on the path of honesty because they know the truth. In the end, character overshadows money, trust rises above fame, and your integrity will always be remembered longer than your product or service. Remember, there is no right way to do something wrong. Honesty is still the best policy!

OPPORTUNITY

Albert Einstein once said, "In the middle of difficulty lies opportunity." He was right. Opportunities are not seen with your eyes, but with your mind. Lack of opportunity should never be used as an excuse for a weak and vacillating mind. Opportunities are all around you if you live in America. Every life is full of them. Every book you read is an opportunity. Every client is an opportunity. Every sermon is an opportunity. Every business transaction is an opportunity—an opportunity to be polite, to serve, to help, to be honest, and to make friends. Every situation, properly perceived, becomes an opportunity. The greatest success stories were created by people who recognized a problem and turned it into an opportunity.

ATTITUDE

One day two men went into the hospital at about the same time, after suffering similar heart attacks. One of the men grew depressed and irritable. He felt betrayed by his own body and saw his affliction as a sign of weakness. His attitude was sour and he cursed his fate. The other man took it in stride. He kidded with everyone who came to visit him and refused to be brought down by his plight. Instead, he spent a good bit of his time cheering up other patients and chatting with the staff. The first man grew weak and frail. The other man left the hospital in good health and resumed his old life quickly. The way we face life has a lot to do with how good we feel about it. If you are negative, then life will be a burden, but if you are positive, life will seem like the greatest gift you have ever known. Your living is determined not so much by what life brings to you as by the attitude you bring to life!

TIME

Stop for a minute and figure out the cost of the phrase "wait a minute." For example, if you earn approximately $25,000 a year, every minute you have to wait costs 5 cents; at $50,000 a year, this figure doubles to nearly 10 cents a minute. If you earn $500,000 a year, your time is worth more than $1 dollar a minute. The point is simply that time is valuable. Every day you can either invest or spend your time. Every morning credits you with 86,400 seconds. Every night it rules off as lost whatever amount you have failed to invest. It carries over no balance and allows no overdrafts. If you fail to use today's deposit, the loss is yours. There is no going back, no drawing against tomorrow. Invest your seconds so that they will give you the utmost in health, happiness and success!

GOALS

Most people don't understand that the reason they're not achieving or getting what they want in life is because their major goals are too vague and too small. And therefore, they have no energy or power. Your major goal will only be reached if it excites and energizes your imagination. It gets you up in the morning. You can taste it, feel it and smell it. You've got it clearly pictured in your mind. You've got it written down and you look at it every day. The great Walt Disney left us many wonderful things: Disneyland, Walt Disney World, Mickey Mouse, the great animated films. But I believe his greatest gift was the summing up he did of his life's work: "If you can dream it," he said, "you can do it." Your major goal is a dream that motivates, drives and inspires you. Think of it this way: it's not what a goal is that matters, it's what a goal does!

PLANNING

One hour of planning saves three hours of execution—unfortunately, most people don't understand that that one hour will be the most productive hour they spend. Instead, they wander into the work place and react to each crisis. And ironically, most crises are the result of a failure to plan. Successful people plan and prepare far more than the average person. In fact, their painstaking preparation can be irritating to those less enlightened. Whether you're in the military, business, sports, the arts or any other occupation, planning is vital, and one of the keys to success. Make a list of things to do every day of your life. Write down five things you want to accomplish that day. Focus your total attention on each task and assign each task a specific time. The secret of your future and your career is hidden in your daily routine!

ACTION

Suppose you had five birds sitting on a wire and three of them decided to fly. How many birds would you have left on the wire? Five birds is the correct answer. Making a decision to fly without acting on the decision is a waste of energy. The momentum to do something about our decisions is energized by action! To become successful, you must be a person of action. Many people "know" what they are supposed to do, but to "know" is not enough. You must know and do. Nolan Bushell, the founder of Atari, was once asked about his entrepreneurial success. He responded, "The critical ingredient is getting off your butt and doing something." It's as simple as that. A lot of people have ideas, but there are few who decide to do something about them now. Not tomorrow. Not next week. Today. The true entrepreneur is a doer, not a dreamer. Don't let your ideas, dreams or good intentions sit idly on a wire. Take action today!

TEAMWORK

There is a story about four people, named Everybody, Somebody, Anybody and Nobody. There was an important job to be done and everybody was asked to do it. Everybody was sure somebody would do it, but nobody did it. Somebody got angry about that, because it was everybody's job. Everybody thought anybody could do it, but nobody realized that everybody wouldn't do it. It ended up that everybody blamed somebody when nobody did what anybody could have done. In today's competitive world, too often people either take the entire task upon themselves or they expect that someone else will do their job for them. And in the end, the job never seems to get finished or is never successful because it lacks the winning ingredient called teamwork. A team becomes a champion when everyone labors toward a common goal together.

CHALLENGE

The killer of human potential is the comfort zone. Someone once said, "Many people have died while still living, because they got stuck in their comfort zone." They became complacent at work, in their marriage, with their health. Our society encourages us to seek comfort. Most products and services advertised are designed to make us more comfortable and less challenged. And yet, only challenge causes growth. Only challenge tests our skills and makes us better. Only challenge and the self-motivation to take on the challenge will transform us. Conlin Wilson said, "When a butterfly has emerged, it can never turn back into a caterpillar." It is up to you to constantly look for challenges to motivate yourself. Use your comfort zones to rest in, not to live in. Use them to relax and restore your energy as you mentally prepare for your next challenge. Remember, if it were easy, everyone would be doing it!

ENTHUSIASM/PASSION

Men and women who achieve the most are invariably inspired by enthusiasm—they approach life, its opportunities and its adversities with this vital characteristic. Enthusiasm is a powerful force that is contagious. Synonyms for enthusiasm are passion, fire and zeal. My favorite is passion. Passion is power! You will never have significant success with anything until it becomes an obsession. An obsession is when something consumes your thoughts and time. You will only be remembered in life for your obsession. Thomas Edison—inventions. Bill Gates—computers. Henry Ford—automobiles. Michael Jordan—basketball. The Wright Brothers—the airplane. Tiger Woods—golf. If what you love begins to consume your thoughts, conversations and schedule, get ready for extraordinary success. Nothing great can be done without passion!

It's later than you think.

Take action now!

Julio Melara

Notes:

Notes:

KEYS TO PERFORMANCE

Notes:

Notes:

KEYS TO PERFORMANCE

Notes: